Doll Crafting Made Easy

The Ultimate Book with Step by Step Instructions and Visuals

Diana U Waldo

THIS BOOK

BELONGS TO

....

....

I can't tell you how grateful I am that you decided to read my book. My most heartfelt thanks that you took time out of your life to choose my work and I hope you find benefit within these pages.

There are so many books available today that offer similar content so that makes it even more humbling that you decided to buying mine.

Tell me what you thought! I am eager to hear your opinion and ideas on what you read as are others who are looking for a good book to buy. Leave a review on Amazon.com so others can benefit from your wisdom!

With much thanks.

Table of Content

SUMMARY

Embracing the Magic of Crochet and Beloved Characters: Crochet is a versatile and creative craft that allows individuals to express their creativity and create unique and personalized items. From clothing and accessories to home decor and toys, the possibilities are endless when it comes to crochet. One aspect of crochet that has gained immense popularity is the creation of beloved characters from various forms of media, such as movies, TV shows, and books.

Embracing the magic of crochet involves not only mastering the techniques and stitches but also immersing oneself in the world of beloved characters. Whether it's recreating iconic characters from classic fairy tales or bringing to life the beloved heroes and villains from popular franchises, crochet enthusiasts have found a way to combine their love for the craft with their passion for these characters.

The process of creating crochet characters begins with careful planning and research. Crocheters study the details of the character, from their physical appearance to their personality traits, in order to accurately capture their essence in yarn form. This attention to detail ensures that the final crochet creation is instantly recognizable and evokes a sense of nostalgia and admiration from fans.

Crocheting beloved characters requires a wide range of skills and techniques. From shaping and sculpting the body parts to creating intricate details such as facial features and clothing, each step requires precision and patience. Crocheters often experiment with different stitches and techniques to achieve the desired effect, constantly pushing the boundaries of their skills and creativity.

The end result of crocheting beloved characters is not just a simple toy or decoration; it is a work of art that holds sentimental value for both the creator and the recipient. These crochet creations often become cherished keepsakes, passed down through generations, and treasured for their unique and handmade nature.

Moreover, crocheting beloved characters allows individuals to connect with others who share the same passion. Online communities and social media platforms have become a hub for crochet enthusiasts to share their creations, exchange tips and techniques, and find inspiration. The sense of camaraderie and support within these communities further enhances the magic of crochet and the joy of bringing beloved characters to life.

In conclusion, embracing the magic of crochet and beloved characters is a delightful and fulfilling journey for crochet enthusiasts. It combines the artistry of crochet with the nostalgia and admiration for beloved characters, resulting in unique and cherished creations. Whether it's recreating iconic characters or bringing to life new favorites, crochet allows individuals to express their creativity, connect with others, and create lasting memories.

What to Expect from This Crochet Pattern Book: When you open this crochet pattern book, you can expect to find a treasure trove of creative and inspiring designs that will ignite your passion for crochet. This book has been carefully curated to cater to both beginners and experienced crocheters, ensuring that there is something for everyone.

The first thing you will notice is the stunning cover, adorned with vibrant and eye-catching crochet projects that will immediately capture your attention. As you flip through the pages, you will be greeted with a wide variety of patterns, ranging from simple and quick projects to more intricate and challenging designs.

One of the highlights of this book is the detailed and easy-to-follow instructions accompanying each pattern. Whether you are a novice crocheter or a seasoned pro, you will appreciate the clear and concise directions that guide you through each step of the process. From selecting the right yarn and hook size to mastering complex stitches and techniques, this book leaves no stone unturned in ensuring your success.

In addition to the patterns themselves, this book also offers valuable tips and tricks that will enhance your crochet skills. You will find helpful advice on color selection, pattern customization, and finishing techniques, allowing you to add your own personal touch to each project. Furthermore, the book includes a glossary of crochet terms and abbreviations, making it a handy reference guide for any crocheter.

The patterns featured in this book cover a wide range of items, from cozy blankets and stylish scarves to adorable amigurumi toys and fashionable accessories. Whether you are looking to create beautiful home decor pieces or unique gifts for loved ones, you will find endless inspiration within these pages.

Furthermore, this book celebrates the versatility of crochet by showcasing patterns for all seasons. From lightweight and breezy designs for summer to cozy and warm projects for winter, you will be able to crochet throughout the year and create items suitable for any occasion.

Lastly, this crochet pattern book is not just about the finished products; it is about the joy and satisfaction that comes from creating something with your own hands. Each pattern has been carefully chosen to provide a sense of accomplishment and pride upon completion. Whether you are a crochet enthusiast or someone looking to explore a new hobby, this book will undoubtedly spark your creativity and leave you eager to pick up your crochet hook.

In conclusion, this crochet pattern book offers a delightful collection of patterns, accompanied by detailed instructions and helpful tips. It is a must-have for any crochet enthusiast, providing endless inspiration and opportunities to create beautiful and unique crochet projects.

Preparing for a Magical Crochet Adventure with Anna and Elsa: Are you ready to embark on a truly enchanting journey with Anna and Elsa? Get ready to dive into the world of crochet and unleash your creativity as you prepare for a magical crochet adventure with these beloved Disney princesses.

As you gather your materials and set the stage for this exciting endeavor, you'll need to make sure you have all the necessary tools at your disposal. Grab your crochet hooks in various sizes, ensuring you have the right one for each project. Don't forget to stock up on a wide range of colorful yarns, as you'll be creating a multitude of intricate designs inspired by the Frozen universe.

Now that you're fully equipped, it's time to delve into the patterns and projects that will bring Anna and Elsa to life through the art of crochet. From adorable amigurumi dolls to cozy blankets adorned with their iconic motifs, the possibilities are endless. Whether you're a beginner or an experienced crocheter, there's something for everyone in this magical adventure.

Let's start with the amigurumi dolls. These small, stuffed crochet toys are perfect for recreating the charming personalities of Anna and Elsa. With their signature dresses, flowing hair, and delicate facial features, you'll be amazed at how accurately you can capture their essence through crochet. Follow the detailed patterns and step-by-step instructions to bring these beloved characters to life, stitch by stitch.

Once you've mastered the art of amigurumi, it's time to move on to larger projects that showcase your newfound skills. Imagine snuggling up under a cozy blanket adorned with snowflakes, reindeer, and the iconic Frozen castle. With a combination of basic stitches and more intricate techniques, you'll create a masterpiece that will transport you to the wintry world of Arendelle every time you wrap yourself in its warmth.

But the adventure doesn't stop there. As you become more confident in your crochet abilities, you can explore even more creative possibilities. How about designing your own Frozen-inspired accessories, such as hats, scarves, or even handbags? With the guidance of Anna and Elsa, you'll be able to infuse your personal style into each piece, making them truly one-of-a-kind.

Throughout this magical crochet adventure, you'll not only hone your crafting skills but also immerse yourself in the enchanting world of Frozen. As you work on each project, you'll feel a sense of connection with Anna and Elsa, as if they're guiding you through the process.

Selecting the Right Yarn and Colors of Crochet: When it comes to crochet, selecting the right yarn and colors is crucial in achieving the desired outcome of your project. The type of yarn you choose can greatly impact the texture, drape, and overall appearance of your crochet piece. Additionally, the colors you select can enhance or detract from the design and visual appeal of your work.

First and foremost, it is important to consider the fiber content of the yarn. Different fibers have different properties, which can affect the final result of your crochet project. For example, natural fibers such as cotton or wool tend to have more structure and stitch definition, making them ideal for projects that require intricate stitch work or detailed patterns. On the other hand, synthetic fibers like acrylic or nylon are often softer and more lightweight, making them suitable for projects that require drape or a more delicate touch.

Another factor to consider when selecting yarn is the weight or thickness of the yarn. Yarns are typically categorized into different weights, ranging from lace weight (the thinnest) to super bulky (the thickest). The weight of the yarn you choose will depend on the type of project you are working on. For example, a lightweight yarn would be more suitable for a delicate shawl or a lacy doily, while a bulky yarn would be better suited for a cozy blanket or a chunky scarf.

In addition to the fiber content and weight, the color of the yarn is also an important consideration. The colors you choose can greatly impact the overall look and feel of your crochet project. Bright, vibrant colors can create a bold and eye-catching design, while pastel or muted tones can give a more subtle and calming effect. It is important to consider the intended purpose of your project and the mood or atmosphere you want to create. For example, if you are making a baby blanket, you may want to choose soft, soothing colors, whereas if you are making a statement piece, you may opt for bold, contrasting colors.

Furthermore, the color selection can also affect the stitch pattern or design you choose to use. Certain stitch patterns or motifs may be more visually appealing when worked in specific color combinations. For example, a ripple or chevron pattern can be enhanced by using multiple colors to create a striped effect, while a floral motif may benefit from using different shades of the same color to add depth and dimension.

Ultimately, selecting the right yarn and colors for your crochet project is a personal choice that depends on your individual preferences and the desired outcome of your work

Essential Crochet Tools for Doll Making: When it comes to doll making, having the right crochet tools is essential to ensure that your creations turn out beautifully and with precision. Whether you are a beginner or an experienced crocheter, having a well-stocked crochet tool kit will make the doll making process much easier and enjoyable. Here are some of the essential crochet tools that you should have in your arsenal:

1. Crochet Hooks: The most basic and important tool for any crocheter is a set of crochet hooks. These come in various sizes, ranging from small to large, and are used to create different stitch sizes and patterns. For doll making, it is recommended to have a set of hooks in sizes ranging from 2.25mm to 3.5mm, as these are commonly used for creating intricate details and small stitches.

2. Yarn Needles: Yarn needles are used for weaving in loose ends and sewing different parts of the doll together. These needles have large eyes to accommodate yarn and come in different sizes. It is advisable

to have a variety of yarn needles in your tool kit to cater to different yarn thicknesses and sewing requirements.

3. Stitch Markers: Stitch markers are small, removable markers that are used to mark specific stitches or sections in your crochet work. They are particularly useful when working on complex patterns or when you need to keep track of stitch counts. Having a set of stitch markers will help you stay organized and prevent any mistakes or confusion in your doll making project.

4. Scissors: A good pair of sharp scissors is a must-have tool for any crocheter. You will need them to cut yarn, trim loose ends, and shape your doll's features. It is important to invest in a high-quality pair of scissors that are specifically designed for cutting yarn, as they will provide clean and precise cuts without fraying the yarn.

5. Measuring Tape: Accurate measurements are crucial when making dolls, especially if you are following a specific pattern or trying to achieve a certain size. A flexible measuring tape is an essential tool for measuring the length, width, and circumference of different parts of your doll. This will ensure that your doll's proportions are correct and that all the pieces fit together seamlessly.

6. Stuffing Tool: When it comes to stuffing your doll, having a stuffing tool can make the process much easier and more efficient. This tool is typically a long, thin instrument with a blunt end that helps you push the stuffing into small and hard-to-reach

Organizing Your Crochet Workspace: Organizing your crochet workspace is essential for a smooth and enjoyable crochet experience.

A well-organized workspace not only helps you find your tools and materials easily but also allows you to work efficiently and stay focused on your projects. Here are some tips to help you create a functional and organized crochet workspace.

1. Clear the clutter: Start by decluttering your workspace. Remove any unnecessary items that are taking up space and causing distractions. Keep only the tools and materials that you regularly use for crochet projects.

2. Sort and categorize: Once you have cleared the clutter, sort and categorize your crochet tools and materials. Group similar items together, such as hooks, yarns, stitch markers, and scissors. This will make it easier for you to find what you need when you are working on a project.

3. Invest in storage solutions: Invest in storage solutions that suit your needs and space. There are various options available, such as plastic bins, baskets, shelves, and drawers. Choose storage containers that are transparent or labeled, so you can easily see and access your supplies.

4. Create designated spaces: Assign specific areas for different crochet supplies. For example, have a dedicated space for your hooks, a separate area for your yarns, and another for your pattern books or magazines. This will help you keep everything organized and prevent items from getting mixed up.

5. Utilize wall space: Make use of your wall space to maximize storage. Install hooks or pegboards to hang your tools, such as crochet hooks,

scissors, and measuring tapes. You can also hang baskets or shelves on the wall to store yarns or other supplies.

6. Keep a project basket: Designate a basket or tote bag specifically for your current crochet project. This will keep all the materials and tools for that project together, making it easy for you to pick up where you left off. It also prevents your work from getting tangled or lost.

7. Label your supplies: Use labels or tags to identify your crochet supplies. This is especially helpful if you have multiple colors or types of yarn. Labeling will save you time and effort when searching for specific items.

8. Maintain a clean workspace: Regularly clean and tidy up your crochet workspace. This includes dusting off surfaces, organizing your supplies, and disposing of any waste materials. A clean workspace not only looks inviting but also helps you stay focused and motivated.

Basic Stitches Used in Doll Making of Crochet: Doll making using crochet is a popular craft that allows individuals to create unique and personalized dolls. To create these dolls, there are several basic stitches that are commonly used. These stitches form the foundation of the doll's structure and give it shape and texture.

One of the most commonly used stitches in doll making is the single crochet stitch. This stitch is created by inserting the crochet hook into a stitch, yarn over, and pulling the yarn through the stitch. This creates a loop on the hook. Yarn over again and pull through both loops on the hook to complete the stitch. The single crochet stitch is often used to create the body and limbs of the doll, as it creates a tight and sturdy fabric.

Another important stitch in doll making is the double crochet stitch. This stitch is similar to the single crochet stitch, but instead of pulling the yarn through one loop, it is pulled through two loops. This creates a taller stitch and is often used to create longer sections of the doll, such as the legs or arms. The double crochet stitch can also be used to create decorative elements, such as ruffles or frills.

The half double crochet stitch is another commonly used stitch in doll making. This stitch is created by yarn over, inserting the hook into a stitch, yarn over again, and pulling the yarn through all three loops on the hook. The half double crochet stitch is slightly taller than the single crochet stitch and creates a looser fabric. It is often used to create sections of the doll that require more drape, such as the skirt or dress.

In addition to these basic stitches, there are also several decorative stitches that can be used to add texture and detail to the doll. The shell stitch, for example, is created by working a series of double crochet stitches into the same stitch or space. This creates a scalloped effect and can be used to create decorative borders or edgings on the doll's clothing.

The popcorn stitch is another decorative stitch that can be used to add texture to the doll. This stitch is created by working several double crochet stitches into the same stitch, then removing the hook from the loop and inserting it into the first stitch of the group. This creates a raised, bumpy texture that can be used to create interesting patterns or designs on the doll's body or clothing.

Tips for Crocheting Small and Detailed Parts: Crocheting small and detailed parts can be a challenging yet rewarding task. Whether you are working on amigurumi toys, intricate lace patterns, or delicate accessories, here are some tips to help you achieve the best results.

1. Choose the right yarn: When crocheting small and detailed parts, it is important to select a yarn that is suitable for the project. Opt for a lightweight yarn with a fine or sport weight, as it will allow you to create more intricate stitches and achieve a finer finish. Avoid using bulky or chunky yarns, as they can make it difficult to work with small details.

2. Use a smaller hook size: Along with the right yarn, using a smaller hook size is crucial for creating small and detailed crochet pieces. A smaller hook will help you achieve tighter stitches and finer details. Experiment with different hook sizes until you find the one that works best for your project.

3. Practice tension control: Maintaining consistent tension is essential when working on small and detailed crochet parts. Uneven tension can result in uneven stitches and a less polished look. Practice controlling your tension by crocheting a few test swatches before starting your project. Pay attention to how tightly or loosely you hold the yarn and adjust accordingly.

4. Work in good lighting: Crocheting small and detailed parts requires precision and attention to detail. Working in good lighting conditions will help you see your stitches clearly and prevent any mistakes. Natural daylight is ideal, but if that's not possible, use a bright lamp or light source to illuminate your work area.

5. Use stitch markers: Stitch markers are invaluable tools when working on intricate crochet projects. They can help you keep track of stitch counts, pattern repeats, and the placement of specific stitches. Use different colored markers to differentiate between different sections or rounds, making it easier to follow complex patterns.

6. Take breaks and rest your hands: Crocheting small and detailed parts can be time-consuming and put strain on your hands and wrists. Take regular breaks to rest and stretch your hands to avoid fatigue and potential injuries. It's important to listen to your body and not overexert yourself.

7. Pay attention to pattern instructions: When working on small and detailed crochet parts, it is crucial to carefully read and understand the pattern instructions. Take your time to familiarize yourself with the pattern before starting and refer back to it frequently to ensure you are following the correct stitch counts and techniques.

Techniques for Changing Colors and Adding Textures of Crochet:
Crochet is a versatile craft that allows for endless possibilities when it comes to changing colors and adding textures to your projects. Whether you're a beginner or an experienced crocheter, there are various techniques you can use to achieve stunning color combinations and unique textures in your crochet work.

One of the most common techniques for changing colors in crochet is the "color change" method. This involves simply switching from one color to another by joining the new color yarn to the previous color. There are different ways to do this, such as the "join as you go" method, where you join the new color yarn as you work the last stitch of the previous color. Another method is the "cut and tie" method, where you cut the previous color yarn and tie the new color yarn to it. This method is often used when working with multiple colors in a specific pattern or design.

To add textures to your crochet work, you can experiment with different stitches and stitch combinations. For example, the popcorn stitch creates a raised texture by working multiple stitches into the same stitch and then securing them together. This creates a bumpy texture that adds dimension to your project. The bobble stitch is another popular choice for adding texture, as it creates small, rounded bumps on the surface of your crochet work.

Another technique for adding texture is using different types of yarn. You can choose yarns with different thicknesses, textures, and fibers to create unique textures in your crochet work. For example, using a chunky yarn will create a more textured and bulky appearance, while using a lace-weight yarn will create a delicate and lightweight texture.

In addition to changing colors and adding textures, you can also incorporate other elements into your crochet work, such as beads, sequins, or embroidery. These embellishments can add a touch of sparkle or a pop of color to your projects, making them even more visually appealing.

When it comes to changing colors and adding textures in crochet, the possibilities are truly endless. With a little bit of experimentation and creativity, you can create stunning and unique crochet pieces that showcase your personal style and artistic flair. So go ahead and explore different techniques, play with colors and textures, and let your imagination run wild in the world of crochet!

Forming the Head, Body, Arms, and Legs of Crochet: To form the head, body, arms, and legs of a crochet project, you will need to follow a series of steps and techniques. Crocheting is a versatile craft that allows you to create various shapes and sizes using different stitches and patterns. Whether you are making a stuffed toy, a doll, or an amigurumi, the process of forming these body parts remains relatively similar.

To begin, you will need to choose the appropriate yarn and crochet hook size for your project. The yarn weight and hook size will determine the size and texture of your finished piece. Once you have gathered your materials, you can start by creating a slip knot and chaining the desired number of stitches for the head.

Next, you will work in rounds to create the head shape. This is typically done by single crocheting in each stitch of the previous round. Depending on the pattern, you may need to increase or decrease stitches to achieve the desired shape and size. This can be done by adding or skipping stitches in specific areas.

Once the head is complete, you can move on to the body. This is usually done by continuing to work in rounds, adding or decreasing stitches as needed to create the desired shape. The body can be made longer or shorter depending on your project's requirements. You can also add details such as a belly button or clothing by using different stitch patterns or colors.

To create the arms and legs, you will typically work in rows instead of rounds. This allows you to create a more elongated shape. You will start by chaining the desired number of stitches for the arm or leg length. Then, you will work back and forth in rows, using various stitches such as single crochet, half double crochet, or double crochet. You can increase or decrease stitches to shape the arms and legs as needed.

Once all the body parts are complete, you can attach them together using a yarn needle or by crocheting them directly onto the body. This can be done by sewing or crocheting through the stitches of both the body and the body part. Make sure to secure the attachments tightly to ensure durability.

Finally, you can add any additional details or embellishments to your crochet project, such as facial features, hair, or clothing. This can be done using embroidery techniques or by crocheting additional pieces and attaching them to the main body.

Tips for Giving Your Doll a Charming Expression of Crochet: When it comes to giving your doll a charming expression through crochet, there are several tips and techniques that can help you achieve the desired result. Crocheting a doll's face requires attention to detail and careful execution to ensure that the expression is both charming and realistic. Here are some tips to guide you through the process:

1. Choose the right yarn: The type of yarn you use can greatly impact the final expression of your doll. Opt for a yarn that is soft and pliable, as this will allow you to shape the facial features more easily. Additionally, consider the color of the yarn and how it will complement the overall look of your doll.

2. Use the right crochet hook: The size of your crochet hook will determine the size of the stitches and ultimately the size of the doll's

facial features. Choose a hook that is appropriate for the yarn you are using and experiment with different sizes to achieve the desired effect.

3. Start with a solid base: Before you begin crocheting the facial features, it is important to create a solid base for your doll's head. This can be done by crocheting a simple sphere or oval shape, depending on the desired shape of the head. This will provide a stable foundation for the facial features to be attached to.

4. Pay attention to proportions: When crocheting the facial features, it is crucial to pay attention to the proportions of the doll's face. Take into consideration the size of the head and the desired size of the eyes, nose, and mouth. Use stitch markers or pins to help you visualize the placement of the features before attaching them permanently.

5. Embroider the eyes: Embroidering the eyes can give your doll a more realistic and expressive look. Use a contrasting color of yarn to create the iris and pupil, and experiment with different stitch techniques to achieve the desired effect. Consider the shape and size of the eyes to convey the specific expression you want your doll to have.

6. Add details with embroidery: Embroidery can be used to add additional details to your doll's face, such as eyebrows, eyelashes, and mouth. Use a fine embroidery thread and a small embroidery needle to create delicate and precise stitches. Take your time and pay attention to the placement and shape of these details to enhance the overall expression of your doll.

Cleaning and Preserving Your Handmade Dolls of Crochet: Cleaning and preserving your handmade crochet dolls is essential to maintain their beauty and longevity. Crochet dolls, being delicate and intricately crafted, require special care to ensure they remain in pristine condition. This guide will provide you with detailed instructions on how to clean and preserve your cherished crochet dolls, allowing you to enjoy them for years to come.

Firstly, it is important to note that prevention is key when it comes to preserving your crochet dolls. Avoid exposing them to direct sunlight for prolonged periods as this can cause the colors to fade and the yarn to weaken. Additionally, keep your dolls away from dusty areas to prevent accumulation of dirt and debris.

When it comes to cleaning your crochet dolls, it is crucial to handle them with care. Start by removing any loose dirt or dust by gently brushing the surface with a soft-bristled brush or a clean, dry cloth. Be cautious not to pull or tug on the yarn, as this can damage the delicate stitches.

For more thorough cleaning, you can create a mild cleaning solution by mixing a small amount of gentle detergent or baby shampoo with lukewarm water. Dip a clean cloth or sponge into the solution and gently dab it onto the surface of the doll, focusing on any stained or soiled areas. Avoid soaking the doll or submerging it in water, as this can cause the yarn to stretch or lose its shape.

After cleaning, rinse the doll by dabbing a clean cloth or sponge soaked in plain water onto the surface. Ensure that all traces of detergent or shampoo are removed to prevent any residue from accumulating on the doll. Gently squeeze out any excess water, taking care not to wring or twist the doll, as this can distort its shape.

To dry your crochet doll, lay it flat on a clean, absorbent towel or place it on a mesh drying rack. Avoid hanging the doll to dry, as this can cause it to stretch or lose its shape. Allow the doll to air dry naturally, away from direct heat sources such as radiators or sunlight.

Once your crochet doll is completely dry, you can take additional steps to preserve its condition. Store your doll in a clean, dry place, away from excessive humidity or temperature fluctuations. Consider wrapping it in acid-free tissue paper or placing it in a breathable fabric bag to protect it from dust and potential damage.

Regularly inspect your crochet doll for any signs of wear or damage. If you notice loose threads or stitches, repair them promptly to prevent further unraveling.

Storing Your Dolls and Accessories Properly of Crochet: Properly storing your crochet dolls and accessories is essential to ensure their longevity and keep them in good condition. By following a few simple steps, you can protect your creations from damage and keep them looking their best.

Firstly, it is important to clean your dolls and accessories before storing them. Use a soft brush or cloth to gently remove any dust or dirt that may have accumulated on the surface. If there are any stains or spots, you can spot clean them using a mild detergent and water. Make sure to thoroughly dry the items before proceeding to the next step.

Next, consider the type of storage container you will use. It is best to choose a container that is clean, dry, and free from any chemicals or odors that could potentially damage your crochet items. Plastic storage bins with lids are a popular choice as they provide protection from dust, moisture, and pests. Make sure the container is large enough to accommodate your dolls and accessories without squishing or bending them.

Before placing your crochet items in the storage container, it is advisable to add a layer of protection. Acid-free tissue paper or clean cotton fabric can be used to wrap each item individually. This will help prevent any friction or rubbing that could cause damage to delicate parts or embellishments. Additionally, consider adding silica gel packets to absorb any excess moisture and prevent mold or mildew growth.

When arranging your dolls and accessories in the storage container, it is important to do so in a way that minimizes any pressure or stress on the items. Avoid overcrowding the container and try to maintain a uniform shape and position for each item. If you have multiple dolls or accessories, consider using dividers or compartments to keep them separate and prevent tangling or entanglement.

Labeling the storage container can also be helpful, especially if you have a large collection or plan to store your items for an extended period. This will make it easier to locate specific dolls or accessories when you need them and prevent unnecessary handling or searching through the container.

Finally, choose a suitable storage location for your container. Ideally, it should be a cool, dry, and well-ventilated area away from direct sunlight. Extreme temperatures and humidity can cause damage to your crochet items, so avoid storing them in basements, attics, or areas prone to temperature fluctuations.

By following these guidelines, you can ensure that your crochet dolls and accessories are stored properly and protected from damage.

Elsa

Color A= Skin color

Color B= Main dress color, usually a light blue

Color C= Color of sleeves and accents, silver or a light shade of blue

With a G 4.00mm crochet hook, work with Right Side Out. Be sure to make nice, tight stitches.

Right Arm:

Row 1: (With color A) ch 2, 3SC in second ch from hook. **3sts**

Row 2: 2SC in each st around. **6sts**

Row 3: (2SC in next st, SC in next st) rep around. **9sts**

Row 4-6: SC around. **9sts**

Row 7-13: (With Color C) SC around. **9sts**

Row 14: 2SC in each of the next 3sts, SC in next 2sts, SS in next 3sts, SC in next st. **12sts**

Row 15-16: SC in next 8sts, SS in next 3sts, SC in last st. **12sts**

Row 17: SC in the next st, DCS 3 times, SC in the next 2sts, SS in next 3sts. **9sts**

Row 18-25: SC around. **9sts**

Row 26: 2SC in each of the next 4sts, SC in the next st, SS in next 3sts, SC in next st. **13sts**

Row 27: SC in the next 9sts, SS in the next 3sts, SC in the next st. **13sts**

Row 28: SC in the next st, DCS 3 times, SC in the next 2sts, SS in the next 3sts, SC in the last st. **10sts**

Left Arm:

Row 1: (With color A) ch 2, 3SC in second ch from hook.   **3sts**

Row 2: 2SC in each st around.   **6sts**

Row 3: (2SC in next st, SC in next st) rep around.   **9sts**

Row 4-6: SC around.   **9sts**

Row 7-13: (With Color C) SC around.   **9sts**

Row 14: 2SC in each of the next 3sts, SC in next 2sts, SS in next 3sts, SC in next st.   **12sts**

Row 15-16: SC in next 8sts, SS in next 3sts, SC in last st.   **12sts**

Row 17: SC in the next st, DCS 3 times, SC in the next 2sts, SS in next 3sts.   **9sts**

Row 18-25: SC around.   **9sts**

Row 26: SC in the next st, SS in next 3sts, SC in next st, 2SC in each of the next 4sts.   **13sts**

Row 27: SC in the next st, SS in the next 3sts, SC in the next 9 sts.   **13sts**

Row 28: SC in the next st, SS in the next 3sts, SC in the next 2sts, DCS 3 times, SC in the last st.   **10sts**

To finish off the arms, crochet around the wrists with color C. Simply attach the crochet hook to the wrist and make a slipstitch, then chain 3, slipstitch, chain 3. Repeat this all the way around the wrist and tie off.

Head and Neck:

Row 1: (With color A) ch 2, 6SC in the second ch from hook.   **6sts**

Row 2: 2SC in each st.   **12sts**

Row 3: (2SC in next st, SC in next st) rep around.   **18sts**

Row 4: (2SC in next st, SC in next 2sts) rep around.   **24sts**

Row 5: (2SC in next st, SC in next 3sts) rep around.   **30sts**

Row 6: (2SC in next st, SC in next 4sts) rep around.   **36sts**

Row 7: (2SC in next st, SC in next 5sts) rep around.   **42sts**

Row 8: (2SC in next st, SC in next 6sts) rep around.   **48sts**

Row 9-15: SC around.   **48sts**

Row 16: 2SC in each of the next 3sts, SC rest of the way around. **51sts**

Row 17: SC around.   **51sts**

Row 18: DCS 3 times, SC rest of the way around. **48sts**

Row 19-23: SC around.   **48sts**

Row 24-26: DCS 6sts evenly over each row. **(Attach eyes, pay attention to nose)**   **30sts**

Row 27: (In back loop only) DCS 6sts evenly over row.   **24sts**

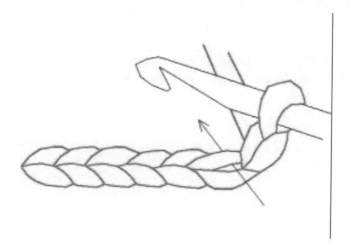

Row 28-29: DCS 6sts evenly over each row.   **12sts**

Row 30-33: SC around.   **12sts**

Row 34: (2SC in next st, SC in next st) rep around.   **18sts**

Row 35-36: SC around.   **18sts**

Row 37: 2SC in next st, SC in each of the next 7sts, 2SC in each of the next 2sts, SC in next 7sts, 2SC in next st. Tie off.   **22sts**

Return to extra loop from Row 27, Continue Crocheting in outside loop with Row 38. Make sure you continue crochet with the right side out and start at the being of the Row 27 spiral. By doing this we are crochet two rows around the neck, making the neck twice as strong.

Row 38: (In extra loop) DCS 6sts evenly over row.   **24sts**

Row 39-40: DCS 6sts evenly over each row.   **12sts**

Row 41-44: SC around.   **12sts**

Row 45: (2SC in next st, SC in next st) rep around.   **18sts**

Row 46-47: SC around.   **18sts**

Row 48: 2SC in next st, SC in each of the next 7sts, 2SC in each of the next 2sts, SC in next 7sts, 2SC in next st.   **22sts**

Body:

Row 49: Do This Row While Crocheting Through Both Inside and Outside Parts of Neck. Make sure that the increases are on the sides of the doll where the shoulders would be. 2SC in each of the next 2sts, SC in next 7sts, 2SC in each of the next 4sts, SC in next 7sts, 2SC in each of the next 2sts. **30sts**

Row 50: 2SC in each of the next 2sts, SC in next 11sts, 2SC in each of the next 4sts, SC in next 11sts, 2SC in each of the next 2sts. **38sts**

Row 51: (SC in the next, 2SC in next st) rep 2 times, SC in next 12sts, (SC in the next st, 2SC in next st) rep 4 times, SC in next 10sts, (SC in the next, 2SC in next st) rep 2 times. **46sts**

Be sure that you are positioning the arms where they would be normally and position them even on the body. If you need to adjust the arms, add or subtract a few stitches until they line up properly. Do not to change the stitch count for the row.

Row 52: (With Color C) Attach 5sts of **Right Arm** as shown in figure A below, SC in next 2sts, (With Color A) SC in the next 3sts, 2SC in next st, SC in next 5sts, 2SC in next st, SC in next 3sts, (With Color C) SC in next 2sts, attach 5sts of **Left Arm** as shown in figure A below, SC in next 19sts. **48sts**

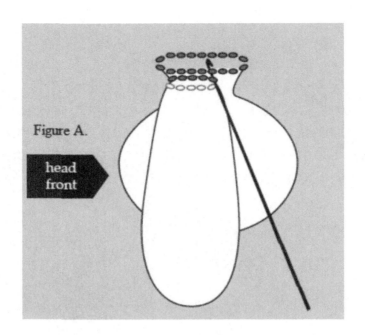

Figure A.

head
front

Row 53: Attach 5sts of **Right Arm** as shown in figure B below, SC in the next 3sts, (With Color A) SC in the next 2sts, (With Color C) SC in the next 3sts, (With Color A) SC in the next 3sts, (With Color C) SC in next 3sts, (With Color A) SC in the next 2sts, (With Color C) SC in the next 3sts, attach 5sts of **Left Arm** as shown in figure B below, SC in next 19.   **48sts**

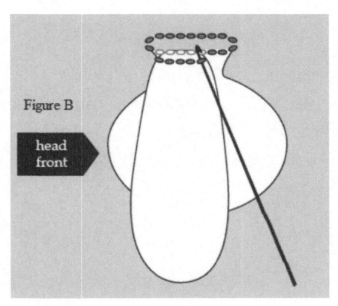

Figure B

head front

Row 54: SC in the next 8sts, (With Color A) SC in the next st, (With Color C) SC in the next 5sts, (With Color A) SC in the next st, (With Color C) SC in the next 5sts, (With Color A) SC in the next st, SC in the next 25sts. **48sts**

Row 55: SC in the next 17sts, (With Color A) SC in the next st, (With Color C) SC the rest of the way around. **48sts**

Row 56: SC around. **48sts**

Row 57: (With Color B) SC around. **48sts**

Row 58: SC in next 8sts, (DCS, SC in the next) rep 2 times, SC in next 2sts, (DCS, SC in the next) rep 2 times, SC in next 26sts. **44sts**

Row 59-60: SC around.   **44sts**

Row 61: DCS 8 evenly over row.   **36sts**

Row 62-71: SC around.   **36sts**

Row 72: DCS 6sts evenly over row.   **30sts**

Row 73: (In inside loop only) SC around.   **30sts**

Row 74: (2SC in next st, SC in next 4sts) rep around.   **36sts**

Row 75: (2SC in next st, SC in next 5sts) rep around.   **42sts**

Row 76-77: SC around.   **42sts**

Row 78: (2SC in next st, SC in next 6sts) rep around.   **48sts**

Row 79-84: SC around.   **48sts**

Row 85-87: DCS 6sts evenly over each row. Tie off   **30sts**

Right Leg (Doll's Right): (This is a continuation of the body, not a separate crochet piece)

Split the bottom of the body into right and left halves, 15sts on each half. Start crocheting the Right Leg with the first SC in the middle stitch of the front part of the doll. Crochet Second SC in the middle stitch of the back part of the doll. Continue crocheting around as normal with Right Side out.

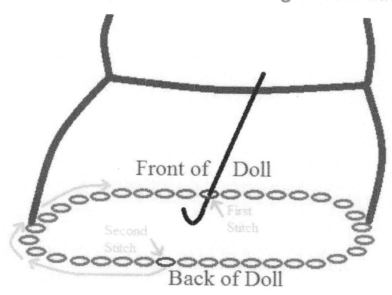

Row 1: (With color B) SC around. **15sts**

Row 2: (2SC in next st, SC in each of the next 2sts) rep around. **20sts**

Row 3: SC around. **20sts**

Row 4-14: (With color A) SC around. **20sts**

Row 15: (DCS, SC in the next 2sts) rep around. **15sts**

Row 16: SC around. **15sts**

Row 17: (2SC in next st, SC in each of the next 2sts) rep around. **20sts**

Row 18-27: SC around. **20sts**

Row 28: (DCS, SC in the next 2sts) rep around. **15sts**

Row 29: SC around.   **15sts**

This is the beginning of the foot! You may need to adjust your crochet by adding or subtracting stitches so that the foot starts in the right position. The beginning of the right foot starts on the far left side (Your Left) of the leg if the doll is lying on her back. See pictured below.

Row 30: SC in next 2sts, 2SC in each of the next 3sts, SC the rest of the way around.   **18sts**

Row 31: SC in the next 3sts, 2SC in each of the next 4sts, SC the rest of the way around.   **22sts**

Row 32: SC in the next 5sts, 2SC in each of the next 4sts, SC the rest of the way around.   **26sts**

Row 33: SC in the next 7sts, 2SC in each of the next 2sts, SC the rest of the way around.   **28sts**

Row 34-36: SC around.   **28sts**

Row 37: SC in next 5sts, DCS 4 times, SC rest of the way around. **24sts**

Row 38-40: DCS 6sts evenly over each row. *Stuff*   **6sts**

Row 41: DCS around until **Closed.**

Left Leg (Doll's Left): (This is a continuation of the body, not a separate crochet piece)

Begin Crochet the left leg with the first SC in the middlemost stitch of the back part of the doll. Crochet the second SC in the middlemost stitch of the front part of doll. Continue crocheting around as normal with Right Side out.

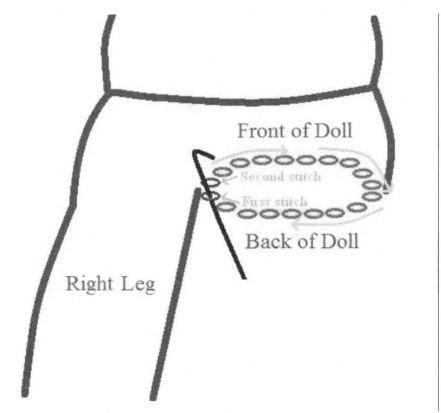

Row 1: (With color B) SC around. **15sts**

Row 2: (2SC in next st, SC in each of the next 2sts) rep around. **20sts**

Row 3: SC around.   **20sts**

Row 4-14: (With color A) SC around.   **20sts**

Row 15: (DCS, SC in the next 2sts) rep around.   **15sts**

Row 16: SC around.   **15sts**

Row 17: (2SC in next st, SC in each of the next 2sts) rep around. **20sts**

Row 18-27: SC around.   **20sts**

Row 28: (DCS, SC in the next 2sts) rep around.   **15sts**

Row 29: SC around.   **15sts**

This is the beginning of the foot! You may need to adjust your crochet by adding or subtracting stitches so that the foot starts in the right position. The beginning of the left foot starts on the far right side (Your Right) of the leg if the doll is lying on her back as shown in the pictured below.

Row 30: SC in next 10sts, 2SC in each of the next 3sts, SC the rest of the way around.   **18sts**

Row 31: SC in the next 12sts, 2SC in each of the next 4sts, SC the rest of the way around.   **22sts**

Row 32: SC in the next 15sts, 2SC in each of the next 4sts, SC the rest of the way around.   **26sts**

Row 33: SC in the next 17sts, 2SC in each of the next 2sts, SC the rest of the way around.   **28sts**

Row 34-36: SC around.   **28sts**

Row 37: SC in next 15sts, DCS 4 times, SC rest of the way around.   **24sts**

Row 38-40: DCS 6sts evenly over each row. *Stuff*   **6sts**

Row 41: DCS around until **Closed.**

Skirt:

Return to Row 73 of body, Begin crocheting in outside loop with Row 1 of skirt. Make sure you continue crochet with the right side out and start crocheting at the beginning of the outside loops where Row 73 began.

Row 1: (With Color B) (2SC in the next st, SC in the next 4sts) rep around. **36sts**

Row 2-3: SC around. **36sts**

Row 4: (2SC in the next st, SC in the next 5sts) rep around. **42sts**

Row 5-6: SC around. **42sts**

Row 7: (2SC in the next st, SC in the next 6sts) rep around. **48sts**

Row 8-9: SC around. **48sts**

Row 10: (2SC in the next st, SC in the next 7sts) rep around. **54sts**

Row 11-14: SC around. **54sts**

Row 15: (DCS, SC in the next 7sts) rep around. **48sts**

Row 16: SC around. **48sts**

Row 17: (DCS, SC in the next 6sts) rep around. **42sts**

Row 18: SC around. **42sts**

Row 19: (DCS, SC in the next 5sts) rep around. **36sts**

Row 20-22: SC around. **36sts**

Row 23: (2SC in the next st, SC in the next 5sts) rep around. **42sts**

Row 24-26: SC around. **42sts**

Row 27: (2SC in the next st, SC in the next 6sts) rep around. **48sts**

Row 28-29: SC around. **48sts**

Row 30: (2SC in the next st, SC in the next 7sts) rep around. **54sts**

Row 31-33: SC around. **54sts**

Row 27: (2SC in the next st, SC in the next 8sts) rep around. **60sts**

Row 28-31: SC around. **60sts**

Row 32: (2SC in the next st, SC in the next 9sts) rep around. **66sts**

Row 33-38: SC around. **66sts**

Row 39: (DCS, SC in the next 9sts) rep around. **60sts**

Row 40: SC around. **60sts**

Row 41: (2SC in the next st, SC in the next 9sts) rep around. **66sts**

Row 42: SC around. **66sts**

Row 43: (2SC in the next st, SC in the next 10sts) rep around. **72sts**

Row 44: SC around. **72sts**

Row 45: (2SC in the next st, SC in the next st) rep 11 times, (2SC in the next st, SC in the next 9sts) rep around. **88sts**

Row 46: SC around. **88sts**

Row 47: (2SC in the next st, SC in the next 4sts) rep 7 times, (2SC in the next st, SC in the next 10sts) rep 4 times, 2SC in the next st, SC in the next 8sts. **100sts**

Row 48-50: SC around. **100sts**

Row 51: SC in the next 2sts, (SC in the next 5sts, 2SC in the next st) rep 7 times, (SC in the next 11sts, 2SC in the next st) rep 4 times, SC in the next 5 sts. **112sts**

Row 52: SC around. **112sts**

This is the start of a small train on the back of Elsa's dress. If your dress does not cover Elsa's feet yet, continue crochet around and adding rows until it does. Then continue with Row 53. If the dress is longer, undo a few rows before continuing with Row 53.

Row 53: SC 60sts, turn. **60sts**

Row 54: Ch, DCS twice, SC 42sts, DCS twice, turn. **46sts**

Row 55: Ch, DCS twice, SC 38sts, DCS twice, turn. **42sts**

Row 56: Ch, DCS twice, SC 34sts, DCS twice, turn. **38sts**

Row 57: Ch, DCS twice, SC 30sts, DCS twice, turn. **34sts**

Row 58: Ch, DCS twice, SC 26sts, DCS twice, turn. **30sts**

Row 59: Ch, DCS twice, SC 22sts, DCS twice, turn. **26sts**

Row 60: Ch, DCS twice, SC 18sts, DCS twice, turn. **22sts**

Details

Eyelashes: For the eyes I used brown 15mm safety eyes. I also added eyelashes to the back of the eyes.

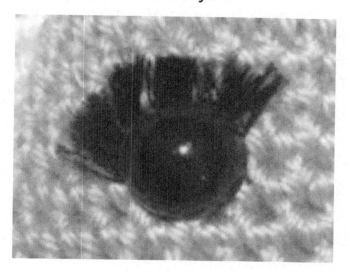

Cheeks: On the cheeks of the doll I added just a small amount of pink blush. This is a preference detail, but I do think it helps define the dolls face. Seeing as I did not add lips to the doll, she needs as much facial differentiation as possible.

Hair: The hair of the doll can be done any way you please. I decided that I wanted my doll's hair to be longer rather than shorter.

First, I cut the yarn to the length that I wanted (36 inches, 18 inches once it is folded over and attached to the head). Then I separated the pieces of yarn by pulling them apart into two pieces (as shown in the picture below). In my personal experience, I believe the more hair the better. Be generous!

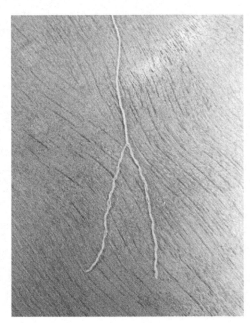

Once I had the pieces separated, I folded the hair in half and attached them to the doll hook rug style. I attached a diagram below.

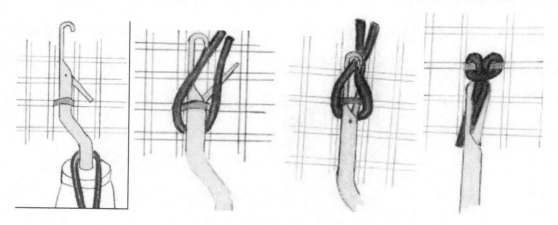

Beading: In the movie Frozen, the top of Elsa's dress is sequined. In order to achieve this effect, I simply sewed blue beads to the top of the crochet Elsa's dress.

Cape: Instead of crocheting a cape for Elsa, I simply made a cape out of tulle and beads. This was much easier, looked better, and gave more of the appearance of an icy cape.

Cut a U shape (24 inches long/18 inches wide) of the tulle.

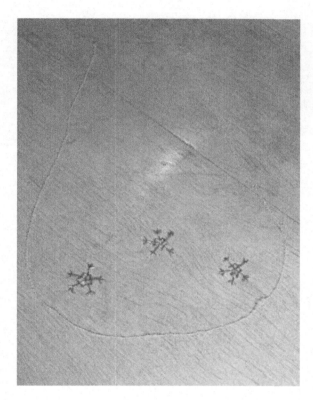

I sewed the edges of the cape with beads.

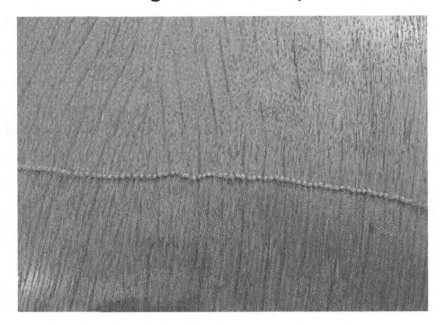

Lastly, I sewed on three small bead snowflakes.

Top of Dress/Heart Shape: The last bit of detailing that I did to Elsa was the stitching around the top of her dress. I simply outlined the heart of her dress by stitching around it with the same color yarn.

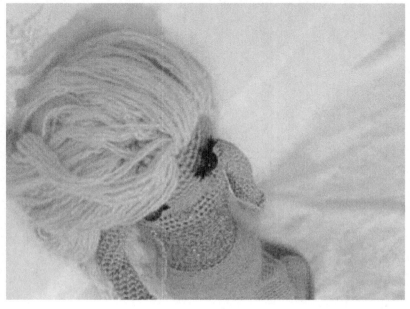

Anna

Color A= Skin color

Color B= Main dress color, usually dark blue

Color C= Shirt color, usually light blue or teal

Color D= Vest color, usually black

Color E= Cape color, usually a raspberry/maroon color

Work with Right Side Out. Be sure to make nice, tight stitches.

Right Arm:

Row 1: (With color A) ch 2, 3SC in second ch from hook.   **3sts**

Row 2: 2SC in each st around.   **6sts**

Row 3: (2SC in next st, SC in next st) rep around.   **9sts**

Row 4-6: SC around.   **9sts**

Row 7-13: (With color C) SC around.   **9sts**

Row 14: 2SC in each of the next 3sts, SC in next 2sts, SS in next 3sts, SC in next st.   **12sts**

Row 15-16: SC in next 8sts, SS in next 3sts, SC in last st.   **12sts**

Row 17: DCS 3 times, SC in the next 2sts, SS in next 3sts, SC in next st.   **9sts**

Row 18-24: SC around.   **9sts**

Row 25: SC in the next 2sts, 2SC in the next st, SC in the next 2sts, SS in the next 3sts, SC in last st.   **10sts**

Row 26-28: SC in the next 6sts, SS in the next 3sts, SC in last st.   **10sts**

Row 29: SC in next st, DCS twice, SC in the next sts, SS in the next 3sts, SC in last st.   **8sts**

Left Arm:

Row 1: (With color A) ch 2, 3SC in second ch from hook.　**3sts**

Row 2: 2SC in each st around.　**6sts**

Row 3: (2SC in next st, SC in next st) rep around.　**9sts**

Row 4-6: SC around.　**9sts**

Row 7-13: (With color C) SC around.　**9sts**

Row 14: 2SC in each of the next 3sts, SC in next 2sts, SS in next 3sts, SC in next st.　**12sts**

Row 15-16: SC in next 8sts, SS in next 3sts, SC in last st.　**12sts**

Row 17: DCS 3 times, SC in the next 2sts, SS in next 3sts, SC in next st.　**9sts**

Row 18-24: SC around.　**9sts**

Row 25: SC in the next st, SS in the next 3sts, SC in the next 2sts, 2SC in the next st, SC in the next 2sts.　**10sts**

Row 26-28: SC in the next st, SS in the next 3sts, SC in the next 6sts.　**10sts**

Row 29: SC in next st, SS in the next 3sts, SC in next st, DCS twice, SC in the next sts.　**8sts**

To finish off the arms, crochet around the wrists with color C. Insert the crochet hook into the wrist and make a slipstitch, then chain 3, slipstitch, chain 3. Repeat this all the way around the wrist and tie off.

Head and Neck:

Row 1: (With color A) ch 2, 6SC in the second ch from hook.   **6sts**

Row 2: 2SC in each st.   **12sts**

Row 3: (2SC in next st, SC in next st) rep around.   **18sts**

Row 4: (2SC in next st, SC in next 2sts) rep around.   **24sts**

Row 5: (2SC in next st, SC in next 3sts) rep around.   **30sts**

Row 6: (2SC in next st, SC in next 4sts) rep around.   **36sts**

Row 7: (2SC in next st, SC in next 5sts) rep around.   **42sts**

Row 8: (2SC in next st, SC in next 6sts) rep around.   **48sts**

Row 9-15: SC around.   **48sts**

Row 16: 2SC in each of the next 3sts, SC rest of the way around. **51sts**

Row 17: SC around.   **51sts**

Row 18: DCS 3 times, SC rest of the way around. **48sts**

Row 19-23: SC around.   **48sts**

Row 24-26: DCS 6sts evenly over each row. **(Attach eyes, pay attention to nose)   30sts**

Row 27: (In back loop only) DCS 6sts evenly over row.   **24sts**

Row 28-29: DCS 6sts evenly over each row.   **12sts**

Row 30-33: SC around.   **12sts**

Row 34: (2SC in next st, SC in next st) rep around.   **18sts**

Row 35-36: SC around.   **18sts**

Row 37: 2SC in next st, SC in each of the next 7sts, 2SC in each of the next 2sts, SC in next 7sts, 2SC in next st. Tie off.   **22sts**

Return to Row 28, Continue Crocheting in outside loop with Row 39. Make sure you continue crochet with the right side out and start at the being of the Row 28 spiral. By doing this we are crochet two rows around the neck, making the neck twice as strong.

Row 38: (In extra loop) DCS 6sts evenly over row.   **24sts**

Row 39-40: DCS 6sts evenly over each row.   **12sts**

Row 41-44: SC around.   **12sts**

Row 45: (2SC in next st, SC in next st) rep around.   **18sts**

Row 46-47: SC around.   **18sts**

Row 48: (With Color C) 2SC in next st, SC in each of the next 7sts, 2SC in each of the next 2sts, SC in next 7sts, 2SC in next st.   **22sts**

Body:

Row 49: Do This Row While Crocheting Through Both Inside and Outside Parts of Neck 2SC in each of the next 2sts, SC in next 7sts, 2SC in each of the next 4sts, SC in next 7sts, 2SC in each of the next 2sts.   **30sts**

Row 50: 2SC in each of the next 2sts, SC in next 11sts, 2SC in each of the next 4sts, SC in next 11sts, 2SC in each of the next 2sts. **38sts**

Row 51: (SC in the next, 2SC in next st) rep 2 times, SC in next 12sts, (SC in the next st, 2SC in next st) rep 4 times, SC in next 10sts, (SC in the next, 2SC in next st) rep 2 times.   **46sts**

Be sure that you are positioning the arms where they would be normally and position them even on the body. If you need to adjust the arms, add or subtract a few stitches until they line up properly. Do not to change the stitch count for the row.

Row 52: Attach 4sts of **Right Arm** using figure A below, SC in the next 5sts, 2SC in next st, SC in next 6sts, 2SC in next st, SC in next 5sts, attach 4sts of **Left Arm** using figure A below, SC in next 20sts.   **48sts**

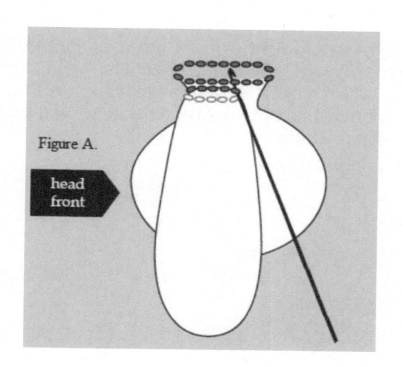

Figure A.

head
front

Row 53: Attach 4sts of **Right Arm** as shown in figure B below, SC in the next st, (With Color D) SC in the next 5sts, (With Color C) SC in the next 8sts, (With Color D) SC in the next 5sts, (With Color C) SC in the next st, attach 4sts of **Left Arm** as shown in figure B below, SC in next 20sts.   **48sts**

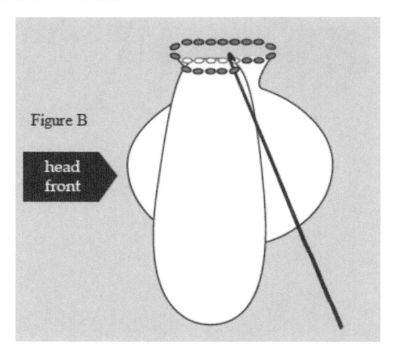

Figure B

head front

Row 54: SC in the next 5sts, (With Color D) In The Back Loops Only SC in the next 5sts, (With Color C) Continuing in Both Loops SC in the next 8sts, (With Color D) In The Back Loops Only SC in the next 5sts, (With Color C) Continuing in Both Loops SC in the next 25sts.   **48sts**

Row 55: SC in the next 5sts, (With Color D) SC in the next 6sts, (With Color C) SC in the next 6sts, (With Color D) SC in the next 6sts, (With Color C) SC in the next 6sts, (With Color D) SC in the next 19sts. **48sts**

Row 56: SC in the next 13sts, (With Color C) SC in the next 4sts, (With Color D) SC in the next 31sts. **48sts**

Row 57: SC in the next 14sts, (With Color C) SC in the next 2sts, (With Color D) SC in the next 32sts. **48sts**

Row 58: SC in next 9sts, (DCS, SC in the next) rep 2 times, SC in next st, (SC in the next, DCS) rep 2 times, SC in next 26sts.

44sts

Row 59-60: SC around.   **44sts D**

Row 61: DCS 8 evenly over row.   **36sts**

Row 62-71: SC around.   **36sts**

Row 72: DCS 6sts evenly over row.   **30sts**

Row 73: (In inside loop only) SC around.   **30sts**

Row 74: (2SC in next st, SC in next 4sts) rep around.   **36sts**

Row 75: (2SC in next st, SC in next 5sts) rep around.   **42sts**

Row 76-77: SC around.   **42sts**

Row 78: (2SC in next st, SC in next 6sts) rep around.   **48sts**

Row 79-84: SC around.   **48sts**

Row 85-87: DCS 6sts evenly over each row. Tie off   **30sts**

Right Leg (Doll's Right): (This is a continuation of the body, not a separate crochet piece)

Split the bottom of the body into right and left halves, 15sts on each half. Start crocheting the Right Leg with the first SC in the middle st of the front part of the doll. Crochet Second SC in the middle st of the back part of the doll. Continue crocheting around as normal with Right Side out.

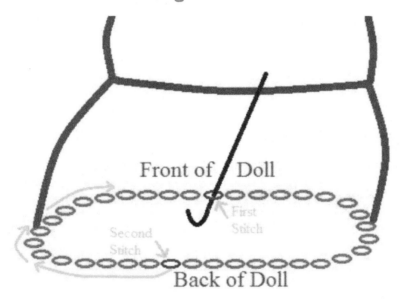

Row 1: (With Color D) SC around. **15sts**

Row 2: (2SC in next st, SC in each of the next 2sts) rep around. **20sts**

Row 3: SC around.   **20sts**

Row 4-14: (With color A) SC around.   **20sts**

Row 15: (DCS, SC in the next 2sts) rep around.   **15sts**

Row 16: SC around.   **15sts**

Row 17: (2SC in next st, SC in each of the next 2sts) rep around. **20sts**

Row 18-27: SC around.   **20sts**

Row 28: (With Color D) (DCS, SC in the next 2sts) rep around. **15sts**

Row 29: SC around. **15sts**

This is the beginning of the foot! You may need to adjust your crochet by adding or subtracting stitches so that the foot starts in the right position. The beginning of the right foot starts on the far left side (Your Left) of the leg if the doll is lying on her back. See pictured below.

Row 30: SC in next 2sts, 2SC in each of the next 3sts, SC the rest of the way around.   **18sts**

Row 31: SC in the next 5sts, 2SC in each of the next 4sts, SC the rest of the way around.   **22sts**

Row 32: SC in the next 7sts, 2SC in each of the next 4sts, SC the rest of the way around.   **26sts**

Row 33: SC in the next 9sts, 2SC in each of the next 2sts, SC the rest of the way around.   **28sts**

Row 34-36: SC around.   **28sts**

Row 37: SC in next 7sts, DCS 4 times, SC rest of the way around. **24sts**

Row 38-40: DCS 6sts evenly over each row. *Stuff*   **6sts**

Row 41: DCS around until **Closed.**

Left Leg (Doll's Left): (This is a continuation of the body, not a separate crochet piece)

Begin Crochet the left leg with the first SC in the middlemost st of the back part of the doll. Crochet the second SC in the middlemost st of the front part of doll. Continue crocheting around as normal with Right Side out.

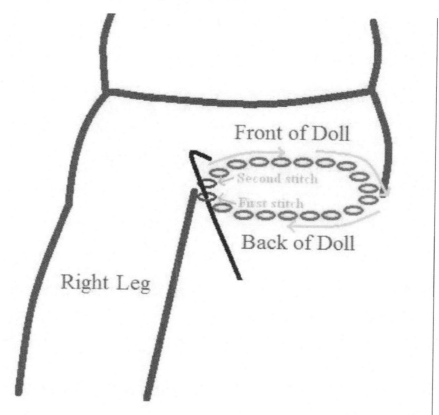

Row 1: (With color D) SC around. **15sts**

Row 2: (2SC in next st, SC in each of the next 2sts) rep around. **20sts**

Row 3: SC around. **20sts**

Row 4-14: (With color A) SC around. **20sts**

Row 15: (DCS, SC in the next 2sts) rep around. **15sts**

Row 16: SC around. **15sts**

Row 17: (2SC in next st, SC in each of the next 2sts) rep around. **20sts**

Row 18-27: SC around.   **20sts**

Row 28: (With Color D) (DCS, SC in the next 2sts) rep around. **15sts**

Row 29: SC around.   **15sts**

This is the beginning of the foot! You may need to adjust your crochet by adding or subtracting stitches so that the foot starts in the right position. The beginning of the left foot starts on the far right side (Your Right) of the leg if the doll is lying on her back as shown in the pictured below.

Row 30: SC in next 10sts, 2SC in each of the next 3sts, SC the rest of the way around.   **18sts**

Row 31: SC in the next 12sts, 2SC in each of the next 4sts, SC the rest of the way around.   **22sts**

Row 32: SC in the next 15sts, 2SC in each of the next 4sts, SC the rest of the way around.   **26sts**

Row 33: SC in the next 17sts, 2SC in each of the next 2sts, SC the rest of the way around.   **28sts**

Row 34-36: SC around.   **28sts**

Row 37: SC in next 15sts, DCS 4 times, SC rest of the way around.   **24sts**

Row 38-40: DCS 6sts evenly over each row. *Stuff*   **6sts**

Row 41: DCS around until **Closed.**

Left Strap (Doll's Left):

Return to the 5 extra loops from Row 54, begin Row 1 by crochet in the leftmost (Dolls left) loop of the left set of loops.

Row 1: SC across, turn.   **5sts**

Row 2: DCS, SC in the next 3sts.   **4sts**

Row 3: SC in the next 2sts, DCS.   **3sts**

Row 4-11: SC across.   **3sts**

Row 12: 2SC in the next st, SC in the next 2sts. **4sts**

Row 13: SC in the next 3sts, 2SC in the next st. **5sts**

Row 14: 2SC in the next st, SC in the next 4sts, tie off.   **6sts**

Right Strap (Doll's Right):

Return to the 5 extra loops from Row 54, begin Row 1 by crochet in the rightmost (Dolls right) loop of the right set of loops.

Row 1: SC across, turn.   **5sts**

Row 2: DCS, SC in the next 3sts.   **4sts**

Row 3: SC in the next 2sts, DCS.   **3sts**

Row 4-11: SC across.   **3sts**

Row 12: 2SC in the next st, SC in the next 2sts. **4sts**

Row 13: SC in the next 3sts, 2SC in the next st. **5sts**

Row 14: 2SC in the next st, SC in the next 4sts. **6sts**

After Row 14, pull the strap over the doll's shoulder and sew the strap to the back of the doll's dress. Do the same for both straps.

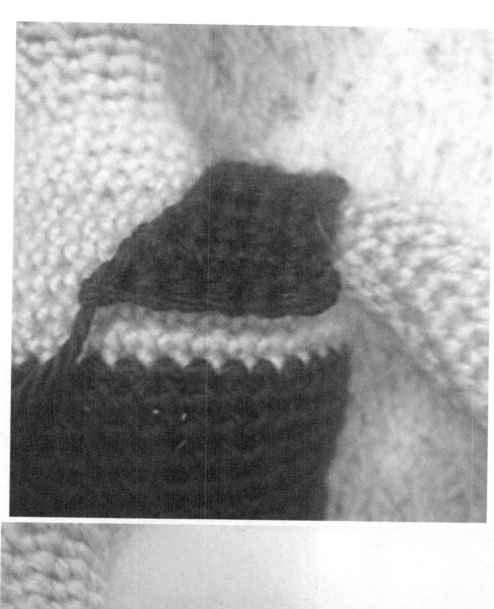

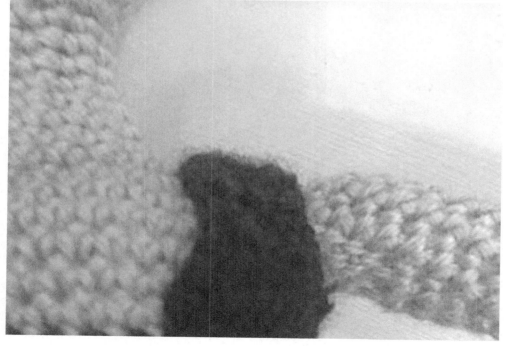

Skirt:

Return to Row 74 of body; begin crocheting in outside loop with Row 1 of skirt. Make sure you continue crochet with the right side out and start crocheting at the beginning of the outside loops where Row 74 began.

Row 1: (With Color B) 2SC in the next st, SC in the next 4sts. **36sts**

Row 2: 2SC in the next st, SC in the next 5sts. **42sts**

Row 3-4: SC around. **42sts**

Row 5: 2SC in the next st, SC in the next 6sts. **48sts**

Row 6-7: SC around. **48sts**

Row 8: 2SC in the next st, SC in the next 7sts. **54sts**

Row 9-11: SC around. **54sts**

Row 12: 2SC in the next st, SC in the next 8sts. **60sts**

Row 13-14: SC around. **60sts**

Row 15: 2SC in the next st, SC in the next 9sts. **66sts**

Row 16-18: SC around. **66sts**

Row 19: 2SC in the next st, SC in the next 10sts. **72sts**

Row 20-23: SC around. **72sts**

Row 24: 2SC in the next st, SC in the next 11sts. **78sts**

Row 25-27: SC around. **78sts**

Row 28: 2SC in the next st, SC in the next 12sts. **84sts**

Row 29: SC around. **84sts**

Row 30: 2SC in the next st, SC in the next 13sts. **90sts**

Row 31: SC around. **90sts**

Row 32: 2SC in the next st, SC in the next 14sts. **96sts**

Row 33: SC around. **96sts**

Row 34: 2SC in the next st, SC in the next 15sts. **102sts**

Row 35: SC around. **102sts**

Row 36: 2SC in the next st, SC in the next 16sts. **108sts**

Row 37: SC around. **108sts**

Row 38: 2SC in the next st, SC in the next 17sts. **114sts**

Row 39: SC around. **114sts**

Row 40: 2SC in the next st, SC in the next 18sts. **120sts**

Row 41: SC around. **120sts**

Row 42: 2SC in the next st, SC in the next 19sts. **126sts**

Row 43-44: SC around. **126sts**

Row 45: 2SC in the next st, SC in the next 20sts. **132sts**

Row 46-48: SC around. **132sts**

Row 49: 2SC in the next st, SC in the next 21sts. **138sts**

Row 50-52: SC around. **138sts**

Row 53: 2SC in the next st, SC in the next 22sts. **144sts**

Row 54-57: SC around. **144sts**

Row 58: (With Color E) SS around. **144sts**

Add or Subtract stitches if the skirt is too long or too short.

Cape (Part 1):

Row 1: (With Color E) ch 5, turn.   **5sts**

Row 2: HDC across.   **5sts**

Row 3: 2HDC in each st across.   **10sts**

Row 4: HDC across.   **10sts**

Row 5: (2HDC in the next st, HDC in the next st) rep across.   **15sts**

Row 6-7: HDC across.   **15sts**

Row 8: (2HDC in the next st, HDC in the next 2sts) rep across. **20sts**

Row 9-10: HDC across.   **20sts**

Row 11: (2HDC in the next st, HDC in the next 3sts) rep across. **25sts**

Row 12-13: HDC across.   **25sts**

Row 14: (HDC in the next st, HDC in the next 4sts) rep across. **30sts**

Row 15-16: HDC across.   **30sts**

Row 17: (2HDC in the next st, HDC in the next 5sts) rep across. **35sts**

Row 18-19: HDC across.   **35sts**

Row 20: (2HDC in the next st, HDC in the next 6sts) rep across. **40sts**

Row 21-22: HDC across.   **40sts**

Row 23: (2HDC in the next st, HDC in the next 7sts) rep across. **45sts**

Row 24-25: HDC across.   **45sts**

Row 26: (2HDC in the next st, HDC in the next 8sts) rep across. **50sts**

Row 27-28: HDC across.   **50sts**

Row 29: (2HDC in the next st, HDC in the next 9sts) rep across. **55sts**

Row 30-31: HDC across.   **55sts**

Row 32: (2HDC in the next st, HDC in the next 10sts) rep across. **60sts**

Row 33-35: HDC across.   **60sts**

Row 36: (2HDC in the next st, HDC in the next 11sts) rep across. **65sts**

Row 37-39: HDC across.   **65sts**

Row 40: (2HDC in the next st, HDC in the next 12sts) rep across. **70sts**

Row 41-43: HDC across.   **70sts**

Row 44: (2HDC in the next st, HDC in the next 13sts) rep across. **75sts**

Row 45-47: HDC across.   **75sts**

Row 48: (2HDC in the next st, HDC in the next 14sts) rep across. **80sts**

Row 49-51: HDC across.   **80sts**

Row 52: (2HDC in the next st, HDC in the next 15sts) rep across. **85sts**

Row 53-55: HDC across.   **85sts**

Row 56: (2HDC in the next st, HDC in the next 16sts) rep across. **90sts**

Row 57-59: HDC across.   **90sts**

Row 60: (2HDC in the next st, HDC in the next 17sts) rep across. **95sts**

Row 61-63: HDC across.   **95sts**

Row 64: (2HDC in the next st, HDC in the next 18sts) rep across. **100sts**

Row 65-67: HDC across.   **100sts**

Cape (Part 2):

Row 1: (With Color E) ch 18, turn.   **18sts**

Row 2: SS in the next 3sts, SC in the next st, HDC in the next st, DC in the next st, HDC in the next st, SC in the next st, SS in the next 3sts, SC in the next st, HDC in the next st, DC in the next st, HDC in the next st, SC in the next st, SS in the next 3sts.   **18sts**

Row 3: (2SC in the next st, SC in the next 2sts) rep across.   **24sts**

Row 4: (2SC in the next st, SC in the next 3sts) rep across.   **30sts**

Row 5: SC across.   **30sts**

Row 6: (2SC in the next st, SC in the next 4sts) rep across.   **36sts**

Row 7-8: SC across.   **36sts**

Row 9: (2SC in the next st, SC in the next 5sts) rep across.   **42sts**

Row 10: SC across.   **42sts**

Row 11: (2SC in the next st, SC in the next 6sts) rep across.   **48sts**

Row 12: SC across.   **48sts**

Row 13: DCS twice, SC in the next 18sts, DCS twice, SC in the next 18sts, DCS twice.   **42sts**

Row 14: DCS twice, SC in the next 7sts, 2SC in each of the next 3sts, SC in the next 6sts, DCS, SC in the next 6sts, 2SC in each of the next 3sts, SC in the next 7sts, DCS twice.   **43sts**

Row 15: DCS twice, SC in the next 10sts, 2sc in each of the next 2sts, SC in the next 11sts, 2sc in each of the next 2sts, SC in the next 10sts, DCS twice.   **43sts**

Row 16: DCS twice, SC in the next 35sts, DCS twice.   **39sts**

Row 17: DCS twice, SC in the next 31sts, DCS twice.   **35sts**

Row 18: DCS twice, SC in the next 27sts, DCS twice.   **31sts**

To add detailing to the cape, I crocheted around the outside edges of the capes. First, make a slipstitch on the edge of the cape, then chain 3, slipstitch, chain 3. Repeat this all the way around both capes and tie off.

Once both pieces of the cape are finished, sew the larger piece of the cape to the inside middle portion of the smaller piece of the cape. When the cape is on the doll, the smaller piece of the cape should hang over the larger as seen below.

I attached a piece of yarn to each side of the cape in order to tie the cape around Anna's neck.

Eyelashes: For the eyes I used 15mm safety eyes. I also added eyelashes to the back of the eyes.

Cheeks: On the cheeks of the doll I added just a small amount of pink blush. This is a preference detail, but I do think it helps define the dolls face. Seeing as I did not add lips to the doll, she needs as much facial differentiation as possible.

Hair: The hair of the doll can be done however you want. For my doll I first cut the yarn to the length wanted (28 inches, 14 inches once it is folded over and attached to the head). Then I separated the yarn by pulling it apart into two pieces (as shown in the picture below). Then I straightened the hair with an old hair straightener. Once the hair was straight, I folded the hair in half and made two braids by attaching the hair hook rug style (diagram attached).

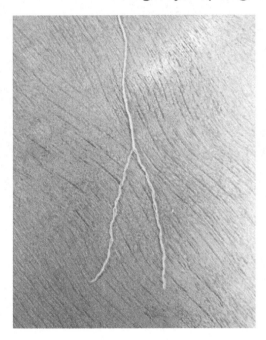

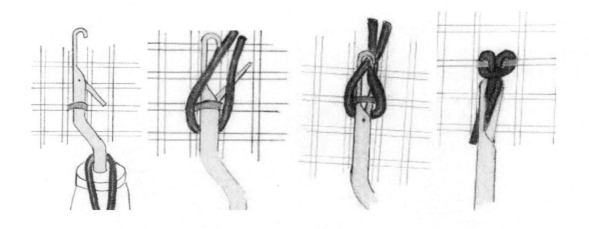

Vest: I outlined the top of Anna's vest with Color E. I did this by sewing in a circular motion around the front, across the straps, and over to the back of the vest.

I also slipstitched across the top of the doll's skirt with Color E.

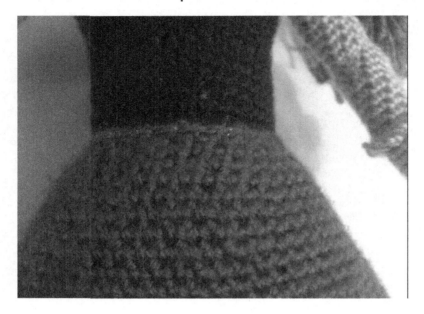

Beading: The beading on Anna's dress is an optional detail and can also be done with yarn or ribbon. The design is roughly based off Anna's dress from the movie Frozen. The beading is on the front of the doll's vest and on the bottom of the skirt.

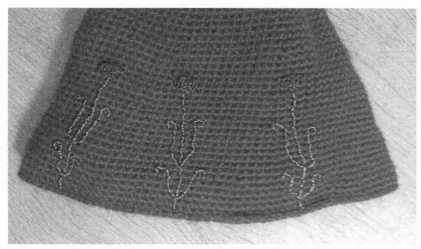

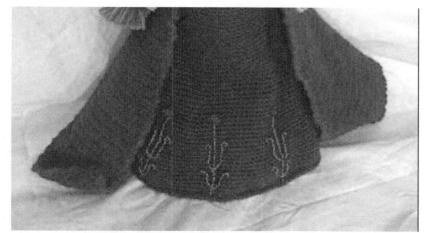

Printed in Great Britain
by Amazon

36229645R00053